ARE THEY REAL?
UNICORNS

by Tristan Poehlmann

BrightPoint Press

San Diego, CA

© 2024 BrightPoint Press
an imprint of ReferencePoint Press, Inc.
Printed in the United States

For more information, contact:
BrightPoint Press
PO Box 27779
San Diego, CA 92198
www.BrightPointPress.com

ALL RIGHTS RESERVED.

No part of this work covered by the copyright hereon may be reproduced or used in any form or by any means—graphic, electronic, or mechanical, including photocopying, recording, taping, web distribution, or information storage retrieval systems—without the written permission of the publisher.

LIBRARY OF CONGRESS CATALOGING-IN-PUBLICATION DATA

Names: Poehlmann, Tristan, author.
Title: Unicorns / by Tristan Poehlmann.
Description: San Diego, CA: BrightPoint Press, [2024] | Series: Are they real? | Includes bibliographical references and index. | Audience: Ages 13 | Audience: Grades 7-9
Identifiers: LCCN 2023000074 (print) | LCCN 2023000075 (eBook) | ISBN 9781678206369 (hardcover) | ISBN 9781678206376 (eBook)
Subjects: LCSH: Unicorns--Juvenile literature. | Animals, Mythical--Juvenile literature.
Classification: LCC GR830.U6 P54 2024 (print) | LCC GR830.U6 (eBook) | DDC 398.24/54--dc23/eng/20230113
LC record available at https://lccn.loc.gov/2023000074
LC eBook record available at https://lccn.loc.gov/2023000075

CONTENTS

AT A GLANCE	4
INTRODUCTION STORIES OF UNICORNS	6
CHAPTER ONE WHAT IS A UNICORN?	12
CHAPTER TWO THE HISTORY OF UNICORNS	22
CHAPTER THREE LOOKING AT THE EVIDENCE	34
CHAPTER FOUR THE CULTURAL IMPACT OF UNICORNS	46
Glossary	58
Source Notes	59
For Further Research	60
Index	62
Image Credits	63
About the Author	64

AT A GLANCE

- Unicorns are mythical creatures. They exist in folklore traditions around the world.

- The modern unicorn looks like a white horse. It has a white spiral horn growing from its forehead.

- Ancient unicorns looked like many different animals, such as goats, sheep, and deer.

- The origin of unicorn tales is unknown. They may have come from ancient Asia.

- Unicorns have a reputation as royal, unique, and special. They stand for purity or rarity.

- Many people believe unicorns have magical abilities. These include powers like healing, flying, and making objects move.

- Unicorn horns are considered magical. They were once believed to cure poisoning.

- In the Middle Ages, people sold objects they claimed were unicorn horns. Most of them were actually narwhal tusks.

- One-horned animals do exist in nature. But the popular unicorn from folklore does not.

- Unicorns continue to influence human creativity. They have inspired books, entertainment, toys, and foods.

INTRODUCTION

STORIES OF UNICORNS

At sunrise, the city spread before the traveler on a golden plain. He paused to absorb its beauty. Stories of unicorns had brought him here. He would soon learn whether the tales were true.

His travels had taken him to many parts of the world. Now he entered a city he had never visited before. The traveler walked through the market. One stall sold honeycomb. Another displayed elephant teeth. The traveler wrote down what he saw.

Hundreds of years ago, travelers would hear stories from locals about unusual creatures, such as unicorns. The travelers would then bring those stories home with them.

In a park near the temple, he found the unicorns. The traveler stared in awe. The tales he had heard were true. He saw a pair of the rarest animals in the world. He dropped his pack. His legs trembled, and he leaned against the gate.

The unicorns grazed. The morning air was still, and the animals were quiet. But the traveler sensed their fierce nature. The pair looked much like young wild horses. One was older and larger than the other. An impressive horn stood out from its forehead. The younger's horn was half as long.

Unicorns are often depicted as elegant, peaceful animals.

The traveler watched the unicorns move about the park. He asked a local man about the animals. The man told him they were gifts for the sultan. The traveler nodded and said they looked like royal creatures. He wrote all this down in his leather-bound book.

EVIDENCE OF UNICORNS

This real-life account of unicorns became famous. It comes from Ludovico di Varthema. He was a writer in the 1500s. He lived in Italy but traveled all over the world. For hundreds of years, people

Unicorns are said to be difficult to find because they can be shy or afraid of people.

trusted di Varthema's account. His tale of seeing unicorns was considered proof of their existence.

Today unicorns can be seen in many parts of our culture. But few people believe they are real. Do unicorns really exist?

1
WHAT IS A UNICORN?

Humans have told stories of unicorns since ancient times. Over thousands of years, the image of this **mythical** animal has changed. Today there are many ways that people imagine unicorns.

Many people picture a unicorn as a white horse. Unicorns are often pictured with a long, twisting horn. People may imagine a brightly colored mane and tail. Or they might imagine a coat with unique markings. Maybe the unicorn's horn glitters or glows.

In many cultures and religions, the color white is associated with purity. Unicorns are usually pictured with a white coat because they are seen as pure creatures.

Some of these features have come from popular toys and cartoon characters.

The white horse with a twisting horn is the traditional image. It comes from ancient **folklore**. But the white horse is just one of many animals linked to unicorns. Across different times and places, goats,

FINDING UNICORNS

Unicorns traditionally prefer to hide from humans. In folklore, they often live deep in the wild. Forests and mountains appeal to them. They live where humans cannot easily follow them. Stories say this was because humans hunted unicorns in the past. The animals were known to be difficult to capture.

cows, donkeys, and buffalo have been called unicorns.

UNICORNS ARE UNIQUE

The unicorn with a twisting horn comes from around 500 to 1500 CE. This period was known as the Middle Ages. Unicorns were a popular image in Europe. Europeans of the time prized them. The animals were seen as valuable and rare. Unicorns are still thought of as special. They are different from everyday animals. Their difference makes them important. A unicorn is not just a beautiful animal. It is a unique creature.

The British royal coat of arms stands for the union of the crowns between Scotland, represented by the unicorn, and England, represented by the lion.

Professor Odell Shepard studied folklore at Trinity College. He explained that unicorns are like royalty. They are fierce and proud, yet gentle. They are majestic, beautiful, and strong. Because of this, they stand out. Unicorns are a **symbol** of special status. Unicorns are still considered rare and royal today. One example is the cartoon *My Little Pony: Friendship Is Magic.* Two unicorn characters are named Rarity and Princess Celestia.

Humans remain fascinated by unicorns because of their uniqueness. If unicorns were a common sight, people probably would not find them interesting. But a rare unicorn sighting is an exciting idea. To humans, unicorns' rarity and difference is part of their appeal.

Unlike most horses, unicorns are said to be difficult to tame.

UNICORNS ARE MAGICAL

Unicorns are sometimes described as fierce and powerful creatures. Folklore includes many stories of unicorns fighting lions and elephants. Unicorns are strong fighters. They move swiftly. They can use their sharp horns to stab their opponents.

People also describe unicorns as gentle or shy. They are often connected to children and young women. This likely comes from ancient stories. In folklore, girls were the only humans a unicorn would trust.

Hildegard of Bingen was a German nun and **scholar** in the 1100s CE. She claimed unicorns would trust noble and gentle girls. They must be "not too grown up, but also not too small, but in the true bloom of youth."[1] Unicorns were often pictured with girls in the Middle Ages.

People believed the horn of a unicorn contained powerful magic. It was the

This tapestry, titled Sight, *is one of six in a collection called* The Lady and the Unicorn. *The tapestries were woven in Belgium around the year 1500 CE.*

most prized part of the creature. Unicorn horns were known for their healing power. Powdered horn was believed to cure all kinds of problems. Drinking from a horn cup would prevent poisoning. Dipping a piece of horn into poisoned water would make it safe to drink.

Today a unicorn might have any kind of magical power. Some unicorns are portrayed as magicians. Others have specific magical abilities. They might be healers. They might make objects float through the air. They might even have wings and be able to fly.

Unicorns exist in folklore around the world. At times they have been considered real. At times they have been considered mythical. But they have always been considered special creatures.

2
THE HISTORY OF UNICORNS

Belief in unicorns is ancient and widespread. Many cultures tell stories about the creatures. But traditional unicorn folklore varies around the world. Different stories come from Asia, Africa, and the Americas. Because of this global history, it is hard to identify one single origin.

The idea of a unicorn is simple at its core. This might explain the confusion about its origin. Animals that grow a pair of horns are common. So it is not surprising that people wondered about single-horned animals.

Several European countries, including Scotland, England, Austria, and Italy, have statues and fountains that feature unicorns.

An animal that grew one horn might have been considered a unicorn. Humans carried stories of unicorns around the world.

WHERE DID UNICORNS COME FROM?

Some of the earliest-known unicorn tales come from China and Persia, which is

UNICORNS OF AFRICA

Several African countries and cultures have unicorn **folktales**. The Ethiopian unicorn lives in the forests and mountains. It looks like a brown horse with a white horn. A gray horselike unicorn comes from South Africa. Sudan's unicorn has a red coat and goatlike hooves.

modern-day Iran. These tales were told before written language was invented. Stories were simply memorized. Myths and legends are like this. Humans eventually wrote them down as folktales.

The Chinese unicorn tale was written around 100 CE. The scholar Wang Chong recorded the story. It told of a unicorn that looked like a female goat. The one-horned goat belonged to the emperor's judge. It helped the judge rule on difficult cases. The unicorn would butt the guilty person with its horn. This ancient unicorn was a symbol of justice and a good **omen**.

Some believe that unicorns can detect whether a person is good or evil.

Another Chinese tale describes a different ancient unicorn. This unicorn looked like a deer with dragon scales. It was also a symbol of justice and an omen of a wise ruler.

The Persian unicorn tale was written around 400 BCE by Ctesias. He was a Greek doctor living in Persia. Ctesias collected knowledge about the world from traders. Traders who traveled through Tibet told him tales of unicorns. The animals lived in the Himalayan Mountains. Traders reported that they looked like large donkeys. They said, "Their bodies are white, their heads dark red, and their eyes dark blue. They have a horn on the forehead which is about a foot and a half in length."[2]

Ctesias's writing was read in both ancient Greece and Rome. Several other writers added the unicorn tale to their own works. Eventually those works were read across Europe.

WHY DID UNICORNS SURVIVE?

The idea of unicorns spread throughout the world in many ways. One way was due to a translation made in 300 BCE. The Hebrew

UNICORNS OF NORTH AMERICA

Early European explorers often brought back stories of unicorns. A few stories came from North America. In Florida, one explorer thought he saw pieces of unicorn horn. In Mexico, another believed he was shown a unicorn hide. Some people said unicorns lived in Canada or even on Manhattan Island, the future home of New York City.

Unicorns were sometimes pictured with the characteristics of other animals, especially goats.

Bible needed to be translated into Greek and Latin. The translators were confused by an ancient Hebrew word for a horned animal. They were not sure which animal it meant. They decided to translate the word as "one horn." The Latin translation

Unicorn folktales come from all over the world. Many places have a local or traditional word for a unicorn.

was *unicornus*. Later, the English word became *unicorn*.

Unicorn tales from Asia traveled around the world with Persian, Arab, and Mediterranean traders. The tales reached Egypt and spread throughout North Africa between 600 and 700 CE. In the 700s, they also began to spread to Europe. Growing and changing belief systems brought unicorn tales into Europe.

New medical knowledge from the Middle East gave the unicorn a place in Europe. In the 1100s, Hildegard of Bingen wrote about unicorns in medicine. Her ideas came from Arab scholars. She claimed that unicorn horns could detect poison in food.

By the Middle Ages, the Hebrew Bible's translation of the word *unicorn* was included in the Christian Bible. As Christianity spread, the idea of unicorns did too. Unicorns became a religious symbol. They stood for Jesus Christ's moral purity.

Dr. Chris Lavers studies natural history at the University of Nottingham. He explains that unicorns' Christian meaning comes from ancient Greek tales. A unicorn's moral purity "rids people of problems, just as Christ rid us of sin; its one horn symbolizes salvation and the oneness of Christ and God."[3] The unicorn's religious and medical roles helped stories about it survive in European culture.

The unicorn is the national animal of Scotland. In Celtic mythology, it is seen as a symbol for purity, innocence, and power.

3
LOOKING AT THE EVIDENCE

Today unicorns are considered fairy-tale creatures. Most people don't believe they exist. But humans are still discovering new animal species. Unicorns are believed to be difficult to find. These creatures are said to be shy. What makes people so sure that they aren't real?

Whether unicorns are real could depend on how *unicorn* is defined. One definition is "a one-horned animal in folklore." That kind of unicorn is real because it is part of real stories that people told. Of course,

Unicorns are usually thought to be solitary creatures, meaning they don't live with other unicorns.

Both male and female unicorns have horns. It is sometimes said they can be identified based on which way the horn spirals.

evidence based on a folktale is different from evidence of an actual animal. Another definition of *unicorn* is "an animal with one horn." That kind of unicorn also exists. There are mammals, bugs, and lizards that have one horn. But there is also the definition of a unicorn as "a white horse with a spiral horn." There is no scientific evidence that this type of unicorn has ever existed.

IS THAT A UNICORN HORN?

Humans have been fascinated by the unicorn horn. But descriptions of the horn varied widely. Some writers said it was black and others claimed it was white. Some said it was white but covered with bark like a tree. Writers also disagreed about other things. Some said the horn was flexible. They claimed unicorns could raise or lower it or wave it around. But animal horn is hard and rigid. There was a big problem with all these descriptions. Most were not based on a real horn at all.

In the Middle Ages, unicorn horns were expensive but available to buy. They came from sailors from the North

STRANGER THAN UNICORNS

There are many strange animals that have been discovered. Because of this, some people say unicorns could be real too. Professor Odell Shepard wrote, "Compared with [the unicorn] the giraffe is highly improbable, the armadillo and the ant-eater are unbelievable, and the hippopotamus is a nightmare."

Odell Shepard, The Lore of the Unicorn. *New York: Harper & Row, 1979. https://archive.org.*

Atlantic who traded them. Those sailors hunted narwhals. Narwhals are sometimes called sea unicorns. They look like small whales with a strange, long, twisting horn. It is exactly like the modern image of a unicorn horn.

The narwhal's horn is actually a long tooth. Most of the "unicorn horns" that were sold in Europe were narwhal teeth. Royal physician Goropius of Antwerp examined one in 1569. He wrote, "I sometimes suspect that this is the horn of some fish." But he added, "It is not absurd to suppose that the horn comes from a beast after all."[4]

Most narwhal tusks sold as unicorn horns came from male narwhals. This is because only about 15 percent of female narwhals have tusks.

Unicorn horns were rarely what they seemed. In the 1930s, a biologist set up an experiment. Dr. Franklin Dove worked at the University of Maine. He wanted to see if he could make two horns grow into one. Dove surgically moved a calf's **horn buds** onto its forehead. The two horns grew together and became a single horn. This experiment proved it was possible for two horns to grow together as one. But it still didn't prove that unicorns were real.

IS THAT A UNICORN?

Many animals have been confused with unicorns. Italian explorer Marco Polo visited India around 1300. He reported, "There are wild elephants and plenty of unicorns, which are scarcely smaller than elephants.

They have the hair of a buffalo and feet like an elephant's. They have a single large, black horn in the middle of the forehead."[5] Polo's description is detailed but odd. The reason becomes clearer as he continues. "They spend their time by preference wallowing in mud and slime. They are very ugly brutes to look at."[6]

MORE UNDERWATER UNICORNS?

The narwhal is not the only ocean animal with a horn like a unicorn. The unicornfish lives in the reefs of the Indian and Pacific Oceans. These fish have a horn that sticks out from their foreheads. It makes them look like a unicorn. The unicornfish's horn grows longer as it becomes an adult.

Marco Polo probably saw a rhinoceros and called it a unicorn. Any animal that appeared to have one horn called a unicorn. But this does not support the existence of a real unicorn species. In fact, unicorns were described as a range of animals in folktales. They were sometimes cattle, sheep, horses, goats, deer, cats, dogs, birds, fish, and rabbits. Unicorns were also described as sea creatures, mountain creatures, and rain forest creatures.

There are many one-horned animals. But there is no evidence of a white horse with a spiral horn. The modern image of a unicorn

The Indian rhinoceros has a single horn on the top of its nose. Some older stories of unicorn sightings might have actually been about rhinoceroses.

comes from a mix of folklore, history, and misunderstanding. Lavers has studied unicorn folklore. He explains, "Unicorn tales mutated and spread around the world until the lineage had a geographic range extending from India to the New World."[7]

4
THE CULTURAL IMPACT OF UNICORNS

Unicorns remain popular today. But few people believe they are real. Their popularity is not based on any proof they exist. So why are they popular? Today unicorns are valued as a symbol. They are popular because their image is meaningful.

MODERN UNICORNS

People admire many of the unicorn's traits. Some traits are valued more today than they were throughout history. For example,

Unicorns are often featured in fairy tales and fantasy stories because of their magical abilities and mysteriousness.

unicorns are unusual. During much of human history, being unusual was negative. But in modern society, it is considered positive. Standing out from the crowd is more culturally acceptable. In modern culture, individuality is very important. Uniqueness is a big reason unicorns are still

BEING A UNICORN

Sometimes people, groups, or companies are called unicorns. This is because they seem special, rare, or unique. If a company is worth $1 billion, it is called a unicorn company. A person called a unicorn has a rare skill or trait. The LGBTQ community sometimes refers to themselves as unicorns because they are unique.

popular today. Being compared to a unicorn is a compliment.

The magical unicorn never disappeared from culture. But in the late 1900s, its image began to shift. Fantasy novels were a huge part of that. Unicorns had been common in fantasy novels. But in 1968 a new kind of unicorn story appeared. Peter S. Beagle's novel *The Last Unicorn* became very popular. It told a modern folktale. The novel began, "The unicorn lived in a lilac wood, and she lived all alone. She was very old, though she did not know it, and she was no longer the careless color of sea foam but

The novel The Last Unicorn was made into an animated film in 1982. The author of the novel, Peter S. Beagle, also wrote the script for the movie.

rather the color of snow falling on a moonlit night."[8] Beagle's image of the unicorn was influential.

By the 1980s, the unicorn looked different. It had grown into a colorful creature. Unicorn toys and school supplies became a widespread trend. The brands Lisa Frank and My Little Pony were very well-known. Their unicorns had beautiful manes and tails. They used Beagle's pastel colors. Rainbows and bright colors were also popular. Unicorns were drawn in a cartoon style. Their coats were covered with stars and hearts. This was a totally different type of unicorn.

Unicorns became cartoons, toys, notebooks, lunch boxes, and stickers. They were marketed mostly to girls. There are likely many reasons for that. But it connects back to ancient traditions. Folklore often linked unicorns to girls and young women. The peaceful white unicorn with a spiral horn trusted them. But the earliest unicorns were thought to be wild animals. At that time, they were connected to men. Humans have changed unicorns many times to fit their cultural needs.

By 2000, the colorful unicorn trend had faded. But it quickly came back with a twist. The brand My Little Pony created a new animated series. *Friendship Is Magic* was popular partly due to **nostalgia**. The new unicorn trend was less about actual unicorns, though. People loved "unicorn colors," which were bright,

FRIENDS WITH A UNICORN

A popular graphic novel series for kids today is *Phoebe and Her Unicorn.* The books were written and illustrated by Dana Simpson. The first one is about a girl named Phoebe who meets a unicorn. The unicorn decides to grant Phoebe one wish. Phoebe wishes that the unicorn becomes her best friend.

Unicorn-themed food and drinks have become very popular in modern culture.

pastel, or shimmery. These colors were used in unusual ways. Rainbow hair dye and makeup designs became popular. "Unicorn food" included cupcakes, toast, and noodles in unicorn colors. Kids played with "unicorn slime." Body glitter was called "unicorn snot."

MODERN BELIEFS

Unicorns have become more of a symbol than an animal. Humans do not expect to find a one-horned horse. But scientists do sometimes learn about unknown species. This is more likely to happen in some places than others. The ocean depths are still mysterious. Rain forests are another largely unknown environment. Many creatures in these places have not yet been

While traditional unicorns are all white, modern unicorns are sometimes pictured with colorful manes and tails.

discovered. Scientists will sometimes call these creatures "unicorns" because of how difficult they are to find.

People's fascination with unicorns has changed over time. But these creatures remain important in human culture. Unicorns are unusual, valuable, and mysterious. They continue to exist in stories and lore whether they are real or not.

GLOSSARY

folklore
traditional customs, beliefs, stories, and sayings

folktales
stories typically passed down by word of mouth

horn buds
the early growths of an animal's developing horns

mythical
based on or described in a myth

nostalgia
a longing for something that is gone or in the past

omen
something that is believed to be a sign of a future event

scholar
a person who has learned a great deal about one or more subjects

symbol
a sign or image that stands for something else

SOURCE NOTES

CHAPTER ONE: WHAT IS A UNICORN?

1. Quoted in Chris Lavers, *The Natural History of Unicorns*. New York: Harper Perennial, 2010, p. 101. https://archive.org.

CHAPTER TWO: THE HISTORY OF UNICORNS

2. Quoted in Odell Shepard, *The Lore of the Unicorn*. New York: Harper & Row, 1979, pp. 26–27. https://archive.org.

3. Lavers, *The Natural History of Unicorns*, p. 70.

CHAPTER THREE: LOOKING AT THE EVIDENCE

4. Quoted in Shepard, *The Lore of the Unicorn*, p. 259.

5. Quoted in "Unicorns, West and East," *American Museum of Natural History*, n.d. www.amnh.org.

6. Quoted in "Unicorns, West and East."

7. Lavers, *The Natural History of Unicorns*, p. 225.

CHAPTER FOUR: THE CULTURAL IMPACT OF UNICORNS

8. Peter Beagle, *The Last Unicorn*. New York: Ballantine Books, 1969, p. 1. https://archive.org.

FOR FURTHER RESEARCH

BOOKS

Peter Finn, *Do Unicorns Exist?* New York: Gareth Stevens Publishing, 2022.

Andy Robbins, *Field Guide to Unicorns of North America: The Official Handbook for Unicorn Enthusiasts of All Ages*. New York: Bloom Books for Young Readers, 2021.

Temisa Seraphini, *The Secret Lives of Unicorns*. London, UK: Flying Eye Books, 2019.

INTERNET SOURCES

Melody Bodette and Jane Lindholm, "Are Unicorns Real?" *Vermont Public Radio*, October 25, 2019. www.vermontpublic.org.

"History of Unicorns for Kids," *Bedtime History*, July 11, 2022. https://bedtimehistorystories.com.

Benjamin Radford, "The Lore and Lure of Unicorns," *Live Science*, June 30, 2017. www.livescience.com.

WEBSITES

Fantastic Beasts of the Middle Ages
https://artsandculture.google.com/story/uAWBn9wmjCVVJg

Google Arts & Culture features the "Fantastic Beasts of the Middle Ages" exhibit from the J. Paul Getty Museum. It is an interactive online exhibit about unicorns and other mythical creatures.

Mythical Creatures: Unicorns
https://artsandculture.google.com/story/9QXxeLPuj4n9JA

Google Arts & Culture provides a virtual tour of unicorn artifacts from the "Fantastic Beasts: The Wonder of Nature" exhibit at the United Kingdom's National History Museum. The interactive slideshow shares cultural history along with historical artwork of unicorns.

The Story of the Unicorn
www.metmuseum.org/primer/met-cloisters/unicorn-tapestries-story

The Metropolitan Museum Cloisters shares information on and images of the Unicorn Tapestries collection. It features some of the most well-known historical unicorn artwork.

INDEX

Africa, 22, 24, 30

China, 24–26, 30
Christianity, 31–32
colors, 13, 49, 51, 53–55, 56
Ctesias, 27

Europe, 15, 23, 28, 31–32, 39

fairy tales, 34, 47
fantasy, 47, 49
folklore, 14, 16, 18–19, 21, 22, 35, 45, 52
folktales, 24, 25, 30, 36, 43, 49

goats, 14, 24, 25, 29, 43
Greek, 27, 29, 30, 32

Hebrew Bible, 28–29, 31
Hildegard of Bingen, 19, 31
horn, 8, 13–14, 15, 18–21, 23–24, 25, 27, 28, 29, 31–32, 35–41, 42–43, 44, 52, 55

Last Unicorn, The, 49, 50
Latin, 29
legends, 25
Ludovico di Varthema, 10–11

magical power, 17, 18–19, 21, 47, 49, 53
Marco Polo, 41–43
medicine, 31–32
Middle Ages, 15, 19, 31, 38
My Little Pony, 17, 51, 53
myths, 12, 21, 25, 33

narwhals, 39, 40, 42
North America, 22, 28

Persia, 24, 27, 30
poison, 20–21, 31
purity, 13, 32, 33

rarity, 8, 15, 17, 40, 48
religion, 13, 32

scholars, 19, 25, 31
Scotland, 16, 23, 33
species, 34, 43, 55
symbolism, 17, 25–26, 32, 33, 46, 55

traditions, 14, 22, 30, 52, 56

unicorn food, 54
unicornfish, 42

IMAGE CREDITS

Cover: © Anna Orsulakova/iStockphoto
5: © VeronArt16/Shutterstock Images
7: © Digital Storm/Shutterstock Images
9: © Valeria Selezneva/Shutterstock Images
11: © Steved_np3/Shutterstock Images
13: © Mad Kruben/iStockphoto
16: © Pres Panayotov/Shutterstock Images
18: © Corey Ford/iStockphoto
20: © Science History Images/Alamy
23: © Jule_Berlin/iStockphoto
26: © Jennifer_Sharp/iStockphoto
29: © Science History Images/Alamy
30: © Red Line Editorial
33: © Jakub Korczyk/Shutterstock Images
35: © T Studio/Shutterstock Images
36: © Corey Ford/iStockphoto
40: © Dotted Hippo/iStockphoto
44: © Mathess/iStockphoto
47: © Pobytov/iStockphoto
50: © Photo 12/Alamy
54: © Illagic Hour/Shutterstock Images
56: © Ivga Photographer/Shutterstock Images

ABOUT THE AUTHOR

Tristan Poehlmann is a freelance writer of educational nonfiction. A museum exhibit developer for many years, he also holds a master's degree in writing for children and young adults from Vermont College of Fine Arts. He lives in the San Francisco Bay Area.